DEFYING ZERO

For Linda (Gene) Armstrong,
    I was glad to
hear that you are still
pursuing your artistic
pursuits —
    I don't know if I
would ever have completed
this collection if it hadn't
been for my granddaughter —
She has material for a second —
    Keep following
your creative impulses —
        love,
        Elaine Lazzerini

DEFYING ZERO

poems by Elaine Lazzeroni

DEFYING ZERO
Poems by Elaine Lazzeroni

Book Design and Production:
Jennifer Heywood Smithson,
Imagine Graphics,
Huntington Beach, CA 92648

Artwork by Robert Smithson

Printed by Edinger Printing
Santa Ana, California

Library of Congress Control Number: 00-090681
ISBN 0-9703715-0-0

for Gracia, Stephen and Laura
who have helped to ease
a nagging Thomas doubt

ACKNOWLEDGEMENTS:

My thanks to Nobel Laureate, Derek Walcott for written permission to use the quotation from *Omeros* as an epigraph.

* * *

Some of these poems have been published in the following publications:

Masochist in *American Poet and Poetry,*

Dwarf, Precision Instruments and Table Talk at Heartbreak House at the End of Compromise Lane in *CQ / California Quarterly,*

On Beauty and *Amalfi Coast* in *Poetry Digest.*

Crisis Intervention in *The Valley Poets Anthology,*

North on the 605 in Mount San Antonio Community College Writers' Day anthology of prizewinners,

Century Plant and *Pearl of Great Price* in California Federation of Chapparal Poets' anthologies of prizewinners,

Crater Lake was printed in an anthology of prizewinners of the National Federation of State Poetry Societies.

Contents

CONTENTS, CONTINUED

CONTENTS, CONTINUED

DEFYING ZERO

"O Thou, my Zero, is an impossible prayer,
utter extinction is still a doubtful conceit.
Though you pray to nothing,
nothing cannot be there."

from *Omeros, Chapter 13:3,*
by Nobel Laureate Derek Walcott

I: THE TREE WITH TWIN-SEED FRUIT

"Why darkness & obscurity
In all thy words & laws
That non dare eat the fruit
but from
The wily serpent's jaws......?"

by William Blake
To Nobodaddy

TREE OF KNOWLEDGE

There
in the center of the garden
was - is - will be
the tree with twin-seed fruit,

Suppose
like the ox, like the ass,
we had looked - look - will look
no farther than the edge
of the eternal moment:
the unconjugated verb to be.

Suppose
the first nagging itch of wonder
subsided - subsides - or will be
subdued forever by craven caution.
Just suppose we had not -
do not - will not - ever risk
the taste of bitter with the sweet.

Then, grass never more than grass
and not one stalk pregnant
with bread and symbolic meaning.
The vine - the grape - only themselves,
lost forever in a one and present ripeness
where no water turns to wine
or wine to vinegar

Without foreknowledge of one's death,
no anxious glance over a left shoulder
at the lengthening shadow of afternoon,
no search of the horizon as light and warmth
follow a swollen sun over the bloody rim,
no awed interpretations of a starry night.

ON BEAUTY:

I know
beauty is indiscriminate.

I, too, have chanced
on emeralds in oil slick
on stinking backwaters
that rival precious lapidary,
carnelian sunsets
in smog-smudged air
over Los Angeles
and Raphael's ethereal luster
in the eyes of my sick child,
the Titian skin tones
of her fevered cheek
made me question
beauty's verity,
authority, sufficiency.

And yet -

one morning after rain,
a light beam caught my glance
and held it on a naked peach tree
to see a rainbow in a hanging drop.
A bird lit on a barren branch
and spread a wing for me to see
a feathered rainbow.

The trinity of morning light,
bird in dripping tree
and my eye's subtle camera
were transubstantiated
into mystic unity.
A trick of time and space
of no significance?

Perhaps -

but what odd chance.
What strange coincidence.
What welcome superfluity.

Two Jays

invade the leafy sanctuary,
usurp the hanging feeder.
Evicted sparrows perch
tense and tentative
in the sycamore's
twiggy periphery.
You might think that I,
old bleeding heart
prone to grieve
for near-lost causes,
would take the side
of displaced sparrows,
but . . . oh!
the jays are beautiful.

HAWK

The strike -

motion sensed not seen,
then beauty and terror
in focus at thirty feet.
Hawk's talons
lift dove's pliant bulk
into slow-dying plum tree.
Gnarled leafless branch gives,
but holds the double weight.

Hawk's patterned feathers -
angular runes, augury of Thor script
light - ripped in storm - stained sky,
sloughed snake skin, fish scale,
fritillary butterfly
and contrast and complement,
dove's mist-morning interdeterminancy,
mollusk, mallow, dandelion fluff.

Prey-burdened hawk rised.
His flight, one sharp diagonal,
scars cream puff cumulus,
horizon's cursive, obscure calligraphy.
Incident and pattern, cycle and singularity
hawk's being, dove's being, my being,
tri-partite consciousness in one becoming -
and my knowing I would not - not know.

BOAT TRIP DOWN
THE SACRAMENTO RIVER

Some tourists fly kites from the stern.
Kindergarten colors decorate blue sky
past Sherman Island, Antioch, Benicia,
Caquinez Straits and into San Pablo Bay.
Traces of children these adults once were
shine faintly through October faces.
Then someone tosses scraps from lunch
to attract a pair of wheeling gulls.

Soon a flurry of gulls dives and darts
in and out of our wake's white foam,
cawing, squabbling over salt-soaked bread.
Kite flyers begin to reel in tangled lines.
Some kites capsize. Our craft tows
dull limp shapes through blue-black water
suddenly darkened by winged shadows.
I think of Alfred Hitchcock's *Birds*.

As we head toward boutiques and restaurants
on San Francisco's Fisherman's Wharf,
I struggle with the shock of self discovery.
I had thought bright-colored kites a prettiness,
had compared the glowing Norman Rockwell faces
to advertisers' soft-sell fantasies,
In the squall of voracious gulls, I found
authentic beauty at an edge of terror.

Past Angel Island and abandoned Alcatraz,
between our pleasure craft and the hazy horizon,
looms Golden Gate Bridge, long-famed
for aesthetics, engineering, suicides.

TO A NOVICE NATURE POET

The lady's not all Mayflowers and birdsong.
When midsummer smiles and faery caress seduce you,
beware of talons armoring those petal fingers.
Though you may string your lyre with skill,
choose with care among your honeyed metaphors,
study the masters to perfect your rhyme and meter,
practice patiently to modulate your lovesick tenor
until your polished song outdoes the meadowlark -

believe me - some sunless morning will go
to serenade your changeling mistress
and find her red-eyed and listless in her bower,
still debauched from some nocturnal ramble
and sullen to be wakened from late sleep.
You'll hear the whine and haggle of a harridan
and catch a fetid whiff of swamp breath
from lips you thought you'd gladly die to kiss.

As her banshee wail constricts your captive heart,
you will know you won't outlive your thralldom.
You'll feel the scorch of her sirocco anger,
the icy chill of her north wind disdain
and learn her lovers' reigns are brief, yet long
to brush away the bits of bracken tangled
in her uncombed hair, pick tufts of fur
and broken feathers from her unwashed teeth.

AN EYE FOR AN EYE

Echoes and after-images
of ritual chants and tribal fires:

"an eye for an eye ...
        I for an I ...
                foreign eye ...

Finger the ancient petroglyphs.
One needs no braille to recognize
writing on the wall, simple and profound
as two opposing camps of stick men.
Cut off from the source of light,
reason falters, vision fails.
It has been said and said.
Said with every permutation,
elaboration, obfuscation.
Some new offense is still
the automatic first defense.
Hit and run. Run for the cave.
Crawl deep where no light penetrates
to paint disturbing shades of gray.
There, in solipsist dark,
one can't confound
one's estranged shadow
with the dreaded adversary.
Between a rock and hard place,
echoes rebound and rhetoric retreats
to anguished vowel sounds,
dumb animal response to pain,
older than the oldest spoken word.
Wails, screams, cries, moans
fade to a puling whimper
as blindness calls for blindness.

APRIL IN GETTYSBURG

I really meant to mourn you, you fallen fathers,
until my fickle mind focused on dogwood.
Mounds of pink and white nestled around
rock out-croppings whose steely blue and grays
were mirrored by the softer blues and grays
of tumbling clouds, and all of it muted,
silvered by slanted rain. It was then
that I forgot the phantom gore and glory
and there was no other state of being
than beauty and the present tense.

Later I recalled the statues and inscriptions
and imagined I smelled blood and gunsmoke,
that I heard cannon thunder punctuate
a clamorous racket of rifle and pistol,
heard fear and anger in rebel cries and curses
and pictured broken bodies all across
the unprotected field where Pickett's
doomed foot soldiers charged the stony hill;
but these stark images would fade each time
my memory shifted to the flowering dogwood.

Was it chance association that led me
to a master's drawing of a garden in Japan?
Black and white news photos? Hiroshima? Nagasaki?
Human forms carbon-etched on concrete?
Does the camera angle of eternity
allow no respite to an all-seeing God,
self-condemned to watch another patient craftsman
carve *"Thou shalt not kill"* into resistant stone,
Or does He cut and crop to focus on one frame
composed of spiraled clouds, a rocky hill
and dogwood blossoms nodding in a gentle rain?

11

Silent Partners

What of the good ol' girls, the ones
who watched them go out with their guns
and had no need to ask them *Why?*
When doors banged shut without goodbye,
they left the *Where?* and *When?* unsaid.
Did the dishes. Went to bed.

When men came home at one or two,
they didn't venture *How?* or *Who?*.
Those wives who fussed at whiskey-breath
ignored the acrid stench of death,
convinced the rules of wrong and right
were clear to them as black and white.

And in the morning when they heard,
they wouldn't say a single word.
With eyes expressionless and dry,
they let some other mother cry.
Kept all those questions in a box.
Rocked their chairs and mended socks.

THE HEALER

for Roscoe Fortson

Black-skinned poet from the south,
language sweetens in your mouth:
hot fudge sundae, honey in the comb.
Minstrel, sing us nearer home.
Cool our fiery inner city,
broken asphalt, sidewalks gritty
with debris of dark despair.
Let us learn that even there,
beneath the crust, lies firmer ground.
With your smooth Atlanta sound,
lullaby us. Help us dream.
Soothe us with your voice of cream.
Anoint our troubled heads with oil.
Gently, gently, still our turmoil
into unaccustomed calm.
Heal with words, Gilead's balm.
Soothsayer, truth-sayer, may your song
help put right what's gone so wrong.
Shaman, showman, conjure-man,
change the future if you can.

AMALFI COAST

We cowards hardly see the famous view.
A hurried downward glance at sea below,
a quick look back toward the way we've come
at houses clinging to the concave cliffs
beneath an overhang, a jutting ledge,
a slender slice of time-eroded ground
between the narrow road and nothingness,
suffice to reaffirm our certain knowledge:
all travel into the unknown is perilous.

My alter ego sits across the aisle,
a tall young man with grim and blood-drained face.
His whitened knuckles grip the seat in front.
Again - again - the tocsin sounds. Each time
the swarthy driver honks the horn, he tenses
just as I tense, both of us alert
and ready to tussle with the nameless angel
who waits beyond the next sharp hairpin curve.

Oh, how his little lady laughs at him.
Of course, like you, she chose the window seat.
Like you, she will recount this scenic ride
in glowing tour guide phrases, seduce him
with a litany of *shoulds* and *musts*
till lured by shame and love he, like I,
will follow twist and turn, descent and climb
of some other Virgilian itinerary where,
cowards that we are, we'll hardly see the view.

Caught in the relentless grip of gravity,
we ask ourselves unanswerable questions:
Do we wish to be more tightly or more loosely held?.
At each roadblock of inward and outward vision,
we are unsure which one should give up grade
to let the other pass - and fear the price
of one wrong guess could be eternal free fall
over the crumbling edge of precipice
toward that open maw, the gaping gulf.

But That Is Not All There Is To It

Recite your poems of doom,
cover your empty canvases
with dark decompositions,
ring doorbells of houses with drawn blinds
and threaten day-sleepers with Armageddon -

Or you can seek out the old men
shooting pool at the Senior Center
and join them in their daily litany:
"The world's going to hell in a handbasket."
It is the custom of the aging,
to sound alarms and lamentations:
defensive maneuvers they use
to protect selective memories
of their *"good ol' days."*

Or you can go to a rock concert
with edgy adolescents and listen
to their lyrics of disillusion
Go as yourself. No one dares
to look behind the masks.
It is the practice of the very young
to waver on the brink of destruction
unsure what unfair requirements
may soon be put upon them.

I too have traveled mean streets,
deciphered terror and anger in spray paint
and knife-gouge on dingy walls,
have smelled defeat and backed-up plumbing
in narrow halls of old hotels.

A raucous crow caw-cawed
near a festering garbage dump.
In its rough voice, I heard
the rasp of truth. But hear me out -
that is not all there is to it.

Just today I watched and listened
to two men dressed in running shoes,
faded jeans and cotton T-shirts
both past their teen-age fear and trembling,
both still too young for Jeremiads.
While they talked with animation,
the one whose T-shirt read:
"International Brotherhood Week"
cuddled his year-old daughter
with competence and caring.

The second man reached for the child,
held her gently a few minutes,
then tossed her a couple of inches
into the air and caught her to him
and joined her ecstatic laughter.
Her downy baby head nuzzled his sideburns.
Tiny fingers reached into the brush
of his ample mustache and tugged
as though she found in those long dark hairs
all the security she needed.

MASK

Empty eyeholes of a Grecian mask
Inquire if I am strong enough to dare
Receive the message in that vacant stare.
Have I made preparation for the task?
Will answers to the questions that I ask
Of Alpha's parent and Omega's heir
Loose noxious spirits in polluted air,
Late-day Pandora opening the cask.
Such questioning is not an idle game.
I tell myself the face is painted wood,
Imago seen through some dead artist's eyes,
No visage of a Name beyond the Name,
Source of all evil, source of every good:
Logos and Chaos wearing one disguise.

"*Beauty should make us paupers.*
should bind us, rob us,
for it does not feed the sufferer."

- William Carlos Williams

CRISIS INTERVENTION

There was more than one
defeated person
in that cluttered room,
more stench than cat piss
and unwashed old age,
a fetid smell from milk
of human kindness
souring.

She reached
one parchment hand toward me,
but left a narrow space
too wide for me to cross.
I did not touch her dirty sleeve.
I had been trained too well.
My job required the tricks
of distancing.

I did not stroke her matted hair
nor dry her tear-webbed cheek,
but not from fear for her -
with or without my touch,
her wornout world
would crumble into dust -
but that the mourning mother
locked deep inside me

might rock that brittle body
at her breast.
For then a fragile tinker-toy
of roles and rules
might shatter
into unfamiliar shapes
and leave me trapped beside her
another lost and frightened child.

JUST ROUTINE

Not even one of the extreme cases,
another one of the ones nobody wants,
that no one has ever wanted,
sits slump-shouldered, opaque-eyed
and silent in the bare reception room.
Who thought it was an act of kindness
to drop him off here at a quarter of five
on a rainy Friday afternoon?

The social worker still on hold
watches fellow workers leave,
then listens to the verdict once again,
anonymous, monotonous, *"No room at the inn."*
She goes to tell him, if he wants,
she'll call the nightline for emergencies.
Perhaps they can arrange
his transportation to a mission.
The huddled shape has gone.

In the parking lot,
five-forty-five early December dark,
she looks up at a clouded sky.
When the wisemen who scan the heavens
are more concerned with quarks
than the quirks of the human heart,
why should she look to the stars for solace?
They have told her stars spin outward,
away from her, away from one another.
She should grow used to distances
and open ends.

He was not even one of the extreme cases,
just routine - and yet she knows she'll wonder
off and on all weekend if he found
some warmth in an all-night doughnut shop,
a dry spot in a freeway underpass.
Or did he curl into himself like embryonic doom
deep in some shadowed alcove of a shopping mall
after the Christmas shoppers had gone home?

A SELF CONDEMNED

Inside his aching rib cage,
the jury sits - his splintered self.
He claims no other peers.
Lids of a blind third eye squeeze shut.
He lives his entire life
in claustrophobic terror between
"guilty as charged" and the sentencing.

His temples throb as a gavel convenes
and re-convenes the court of justice.
Somewhere near the base of his skull,
a black-robed judge stirs, yawns
and nods off once again - bored
with the testimony's banality.
This case will not make legal history.

Just below his navel, poisonous fumes
rumble, the prosecution's summary -
too full of his own bile and choler
to be ignored as circumstantial.
At the base of his spine, curled
in fetal impotence, the counsel for defense
babbles incoherently.

Blindfold askew, the leering lady winks,
mocks him with a knowing smile,
forces his attention toward the scales
weighted with damning evidence:
everything he has put his hand to
smudged with identifiable fingerprints,
his undeniable script - openly confessional.

SWEET GIRL BRIDE

The checks come back
from the last board and care.
She has tricked them again,
spit out the lithium
and fled into her fantasy.

The State and County
in unholy matrimony,
blessed by no sacraments
other than federal codes
and shrinking budgets,

parent her and the child
she would not claim.
That could not be her baby.
She was chaste, a virgin.
Might become a nun.

Her conservator
and the social worker
find no trace until
the anguished phone call
from a parish priest:

"A church is sanctuary -
BUT sodden underwear
spread in the restroom,
half-cooked chicken
near the vigil lights . . . ?"

The new trail leads them
to the garment district,
an ill-lit full length mirror,
a dirty barefoot woman-child
in a long white wedding dress.

After Babel

A little past Hope Street
going east on Seventh ,
a ragget prophet shouts:

YOU ARE ALL GOING TO HELL!

Towers obscure the public library
and the site of the old landmark,
the church with the JESUS SAVES sign.
On a bright-sun Santana day,
it is chilly in the shadowed
corridor between tall buildings.
Scantily clad, *Poor Tom* shivers
toward Grand and shouts:

YOU ARE ALL GOING TO HELL!

He stops at the intersection,
not so far gone he can't tell
red from green or see significance
in the international symbols.
The crowd presses about him, surges
seconds before the light change.
Restrained by the small red hand of God,
he stands on the curb and shouts:

YOU ARE ALL GOING TO HELL!

Shepherded by the little green man,
he crosses slowly with the the chirp-chirp.
his worn sandals slap toward Olive - Hill -
Again and again, the hoarse voice shouts:

YOU ARE ALL GOING TO HELL!

The crowd ignores him, gives
what little space it can
to one more L.A. eccentric.
Perhaps the multilingual multitudes
have not yet learned sufficient English
to understand him.

PARK BENCH PHILOSOPHER

"I am no teacher", the old man says,
    "But this much I can tell you:
    there is dying in should not,
    lying in could not,
    folly in would not -

and these are poisonous truths,
    not just boastful bragging,
    but addictive drugs and harmful stimulants,
    and meat for censorship for those who censor -
    so send the kiddies to the playground.

If your grown-up belly is strong enough
    to learn of my exotic dishes
    and stay on your own diet,
    I'll tell you stories - now hear me right -
    not lessons life has taught me - stories

of the orgies of illogic where I danced,
    and how I came back drunk and weary,
    crawled into my cave to sleep it off
    and woke refreshed and hungry - so hungry
    I ate a rat I'd skinned and boiled.

That cooked-dead rat gnawed me as I swallowed
    and all my retching could not loose it.
    As it travelled slowly through my guts,
    it gnawed and chewed and gnawed -
    but that has passed or I have passed it."

Let's sit and swap stories" , the old man says,
    "but send the kiddies out of earshot.
    An old man's honest mind is no amusement park.
    Let them go climb the jungle gym, grow strong enough
    they may survive jungles such as I have known."

TABLE TALK IN HEARTBREAK HOUSE
AT THE END OF COMPROMISE LANE

They talk a lot of cabbages and kings.
There is no substance in the words they say.
They cannot face the more important things.

This litany of harmless happenings
will scarcely scar the surface of the day.
They will talk a lot of cabbages and kings.

They hide in platitudes and posturings.
The time they share is easier that way.
They cannot face the more important things.

Their memories are wasps with wicked stings
They chase thrm off. They dare not let them stay.
They talk a lot of cabbages and kings.

A thoughtless break in weak defenses brings
back images of grief they've stored away.
They cannot face the more important things.

These empty nothings are their offerings
to household gods to keep the truth at bay.
They talk a lot of cabbages and kings.
They cannot face the more important things.

GLUTTON

He would
if he could
ingest the world,
bolt the whole banquet
course after unnumbered course
napkin tucked in collar
knife in his right hand
fork in his left
efficient European style -

or even more efficient
like an ancient noble
at the festive board
in a smoky torch-lit hall,
tear the joint bare-handed
suck the marrow
mop juices with a crust
eyeing his neighbor's portion
as he licks his sticky fingers.

At a smorgasbord of choices
with indiscriminate hunger
more intense than appetite,
he will chance it all
sweet salt sour bitter,
spit out pits and rinds
he finds too tough

Condemned to guily greed
locked in the confines
of an unmet need,
he dares not question
whose last supper
the tolling bell
announces.

IN A SUPERMARKET

I saw her in a produce section piled
with artful pyramids of summer fruit,
a narrow-chested youngster big with child
pushing a heavy basket with a cute,
but grubby, baby in the infant seat,
and clinging to her side, a girl not four
who got down on her hands and knees to eat
grapes fallen from the counter to the floor.

When that young mother scanned the rich display,
her dawn-fresh eyes considering a crop
where nothing is forbidden if you pay,
I watched her sigh, then shake her head and stop,
collect her sticky child and push her load
of cereal and such on down the aisle.
My choices made, I paid my bill and rode
back home to decorate my kitchen tile.

I built a still life on a footed plate
with peaches plump as breasts of nursing mothers,
some scarlet grapes in pendant clusters, great
blue-purple plums and golden pears like others
on museum walls where darkened grounds
are lit by glowing pigments. I felt no pride
in my creation. It was out of bounds
to dote upon a fraud. I could not hide

the knowledge all was counterfeited ripeness.
Picked green and summer faked by storeroom heat,
I knew my stillborn sculpture to be tasteless
with wax and dye concealing spoiling meat.
I turned in sorrow but I did not grieve
for blighted fruit. The summer afternoon
was haunted by an undernourished Eve
evicted from the garden much too soon.

AT A CORNER CROSSING

You have seen them
near a busy intersection,
mother and child.
No Raphael *Madonna*,
this pale young woman
gaunt as Donatello's *Magdalen*.
No Rubens' plump pink cherub,
this scrawny, scabby child.
The woman's skeletal
right forearm reaches out,
empty palm turned up.
Dull eyes stare
into Sunday traffic.
The child beside her
is so young she has not yet
forgotten how to cry.
Have you seen the woman's
left hand touch, then cradle
the child's small hand
in a nest of bony fingers?
In her downward glance
at the tear-streaked face,
did you catch the sheen
of end-of-summer plants
rinsed mid-March clean
by a sudden autumn shower,
the tender toughness
of dusty toxic oleander
buffeted by backwind
from passing cars?

PALM MOTEL

An ironic name for this treeless place.
Even the patchy devil grass edging
the gravel driveway doesn't look too robust.
Floaters, end-of-the-roaders, can rent
forlorn bungalows by the hour - by the mouth.
There are a half-dozen old-timers,
regulars as close as family, and on hot days,
(the air conditioners failed long ago)
the manager who gets free rent for maintenance
sits with them in the narrow shade
to drink beer and gab or merely doze.

Torn screens, rips in thin paper blinds,
scabrous paint can wait till the mercury drops
in the thermometer on the office wall.
Then, of course, rainy days, near-zero days
aren't good work days either and maintenance
can wait out daytime soaps, old sit-com re-runs
and the vicarious passion on talk shows.
The TV is the one thing here that gets repaired.
"This place ain't so bad." he'll say.
*"It's a step up from that flea-ridden
trailer park half-a-mile down the road."*

The name there is Mar Vista although for years
the only view has been the graffiti-d
block wall dividing the road from the freeway.
Does it help that absentee owners hang on
to romantic names for these rundown places?
Does some false memory of faded glamour
block the irrelevance of flashy TV ads,
close out images of shapeless figures pushing
shopping carts filled with lumpy plastic bags
and the fear that this could be the last stop
before seeking nameless numberless shelter?

KEYS

When old folks go
they leave behind
odd-sized odd-shaped
keys

on key rings
with tarnished
St. Christopher
medals

loose in dresser drawers
on yellowed newsprint
beneath darned socks
and faded underwear

tied to shoestrings
looped over rusted nails
in musty closets
by torn screen doors

knotted into handkerchiefs
inside linty pockets
of dark wool suits
and winter greatcoats

in dented tin boxes
with scratched lids
in false bottoms
of steamer trunks

no one can find
locks they fit
to open secret doors
and buried treasure chests

HOME CALLS IN THE SIXTIES

Two companion pictures on the wall;
the sad-eyed Jesus of the bleeding heart
and the bright-haired fallen president,
bungalow after bungalow
all through San Gabriel Valley.
These mourners did not know how far
he was from sainthood. They only knew,
flawed like themselves, he was no saint
and thought no less of him for that.
Felt close to him for all the distance
the wealth the fame the power
knowing he too had stood before the altar
the transformed wafer melting on his tongue,
stood emptied of the last transgression
cleansed by the solemn voice, the curtained face
in the carved wood box of the confessional.
Knew, like a drunken favorite uncle
like a gunned-down younger brother
like the sunny choir boy child
turned sullen withdrawn son,
he too had gambled on long life
and deathbed absolution
and lost.

MIXED BLESSINGS

<u>Definitions:</u>

The Readers' Digest
Great Encyclopedia Dictionary, 1966
        <u>blessing</u>:   #1. an invocation or declaration
                                   of divine favor, benediction
                         #6. a cursing or scolding

Webster's New Twentieth Century Dictionary
of the English Language, Second Edition, 1979
        <u>blessing</u>:   #1. benediction
                         #8. a cursing or scolding

The New Shorter Oxford English Dictionary,
Clarendon Press, Oxford, England, 1993
        <u>to bless:</u>   #1. invoke divine favor
                         #7. pronounce an imprecation upon,
                                   curse, damn (colloq.)

Bless´ed is the State Legislature
for prohibiting re-use of food
left on restaurant tables
and alleys with garbage dumpsters
teeming with more nutrition
than whiskered long-tailed rats
can eat by themselves.

Bless´ed are highway engineers
who weave congested traffic lanes
into cloverleaves with cubbyholes,
shallow caves beside the underpasses
where squatter communes recycle
cardboard box and plastic sheet
from litter to private property

Bless´ed are absentee landlords
of drafty ill-lit hotels
with shifty-eyed desk clerks
where a county voucher buys
a night of uneasy sleep
on rusted bedsprings barely covered
by a stained and sheetless mattress.

Bless´ed are doughnut franchises
that stay open 24 hours,
where the ones who do not make
the final cut through red tape
can dry out on a rainy night,
perhaps get lucky, find an inch or two
of lukewarm coffee in a paper cup.

Bless´ed are weedy trailer parks
with scabby kids and mangy dogs
where a southern gentleman
in a sodden three-piece suit
can lie in his urine and vomit, curse,
quote *King James* and cry for his mother,
unnoticed and undisturbed.

Bless´ed is the vodka stupor
that lets you get past the alcoholic,
immobile in front of a rolling TV,
and into the cramped bed space
of the sixteen-foot house trailer
to find his bedfast wife,
unconscious and dehydrated.

Bless'ed are property-proud neighbors
concerned that rats may prowl
through untrimmed weeds next door,
who alert you to an elder sister,
wheelchair bound, who will not break
the deathbed vow she made her mother
to care for a demented younger sister.

Bless'ed is the Mental Health examiner
who tells you senses of the human species
are adaptable: how, if you can stand
the first ten minutes of soured milk cartons,
unwashed cat food tins, mounds of cat shit
in the corners of the cobwebbed dining room,
the stench will seem to lesson.

Bless'ed is the board-and-care home
with a live-in manager and wife,
no more and no less dysfunctional
than the boarders, who live as family,
no less and no more dysfunctional,
than the family which spawned
and spurned each one of them.

Bless'ed are convalescent homes
where ammoniated air greets one
at the door, who admit another
patient into over-crowded halls
before the card from *Medicaid* is issued,
and do not ask the foreign janitors
and nurses' aides to show their green cards.

Bless´ed is the owner-doctor
who signs medical charts
without leaving the nurses' station,
a month's work of patient contacts
completed during lunch hour, grants
another month of dubious care to patients
whose disability is nowhere else to go.

Bless´ed are the cool clean sheets
in the psychiatric wing
of the over-crowded county hospital,
for the inmate's 72-hour reprieve
from her family of "poisoners,"
for the distraught family's
72-hour reprieve from loving hell.

Bless´ed is the office clown
undaunted by extremes of human behavior,
whose skill at black humor
can turn the latest horror story
into a stand-up comedy routine,
who knows shared laughter
can lighten a heavy workload.

Bless´ed is the seasoning that helps
you learn you have no loaves and fishes
to feed the hungry multitudes,
no skill to make the paralytic walk,
the blind man see, or free
the schizophrenic from his devils
by changing them to fleeing swine.

Bles´sed are reluctant taxpayers
and shrinking county budgets,
administrative memos, regulations
that keep the cases moving,
so you don't know if bandages
stay put on walking wounded, how soon
a smoldering hot spot re-ignites.

Bless´ed are Friday afternoons
and weekends at home, although
you know whose auras and vibrations
came home with you all week.
Why should you be surprised
if disenfranchised shades
begin to clamor for co-tenancy?

III. WAVING THROUGH A HALF-CLOSED WINDOW

" *And whoever walks a furlong*
without sympathy
walks to his own funeral
drest in his shroud. "

Song of Myself
by Walt Whitman

"*Not for a moment Walt Whitman*
comely old man,
have I ceased to envision
your beard full of butterflies. "

Poet in New York
by Federico Garcia Lorc

DWARF

In a gait almost a swagger,
you cross six lanes of traffic.
Arms swing hard, urge wizened legs
to take yet one more giant step.

What careless craft foreshortened you,
scrambled patterns to cut you on this bias?
What dropped stitch in embryonic time
left you mismatched and top-heavy?

Walk proud in front of my stopped car.
I don't laugh at side shows or old films
when your slapstick double skitters
from some pompous cop he's tripped.

The world no longer gives you cap and bells
or lets you nestle in a king's soft lap
to tickle his fat sides with needle wit
until split doublet bares a royal nakedness.

Were those tiny faded denims
purchased at a childrens' shop?
Did someone's patient hands rip seams
and alter kindergarten garments?

I hope where you are headed
there is a woman who will listen
when you share a grown man's thoughts
that match your muscled arms.

BENEFICIARY

He cannot count to ten and never will.
Always takes the nickel, not the dime,
its heft more solid in his pudgy hand,
He shakes the bank again, again, again
to hear the *pizzicato* of the coins.

The alchemists were wrong.
The secret of wealth is time, not gold.
Time - he spends great chunks of it
lying on his back beneath a tree
entranced by breeze-blown leaves
scissoring odd-shaped bits of sky.

Or he unties, ties, unties, ties his shoelaces.
Each time his stubby fingers make a loop,
he sits a while, grins at his handiwork
before he brings the other lace around.
He makes a second loop and stares
at the first, the second, back at the first.

For him nothing is cumulative,
each moment shines unique and eternal,
with no closure, no ominous deadline,
one unfolding now untroubled by absence.
When he holds the pocket watch left to him
by his fast-forgotten father,

his finger traces clouds, trees, stag -
then the motto inside the cover,
unaware and unconcerned the letters spell
Tempus Fugit not *Aeternitas*. He does not lift
the lid to track the passing hour, but to hear
the tinkling tune the golden timepiece plays.

CENTURY PLANT

She grows tough leaves.
Each leaf honed
to razor edge and saber point
to keep out passers-by
who come too close
too soon.

Ascetic by nature
not by choice,
she lives her inward life alone.
No devil comes to tempt her
from her wilderness.
No angel comes to prophesy.

Through long hot days of sun,
through long cold starshine nights,
her need to love grows concentrate.
She pushes yearning seed
up through one towering stem
and gives a flower to the sky.

Namedropper

How glibly the semi-private nickname
glides from the testifying tongue.
For all the air of implied intimacy,
this utterance is far from casual.
Mantra-like, naming and re-naming
invoke the moment's reoccurence:
the brushed sleeve, the touched hem,
a fragment self made whole and holy
by satellite shine of borrowed being -
an autograph, a yellowed clipping,
a sweated handkerchief pocketed
played close to the chest
like a good hand of chance-dealt cards.

FORTRESS

She has turned herself inside out,
hung pieces of herself on every wall,
turned memory's heavy pockets onto table tops.
Emptied - these tokens do her grieving.
>*Let raw-nerved trinkets bleed.*
>*Let faded photos weep.*
She can not cry, not any more.

Armored and dry-eyed, she sits on guard
among the children of the past.
When children of today with careless hands
threaten fragile treasures,
here gentle voice unsheathes its underside,
>a sharp-edged mason's tool
>reinforces unseen barriers:
Why must they bring their children here?

Sound waves creep along thin wires,
pierce the laden walls - a flank attack,
her other son's familiar voice.
>The tokens tremble.
>She asks too much.
Still she will not cry - not now - not yet.

She does not say his name, parries his *Hello, Mom,*
disarms him with her *Hello, stranger -*
>reminds him once again,
>he never knew the password.

Narrow Gauge Train To Limón

Past the ridge the track uncurls,
strikes for the Carib coast.
Jungle gnaws on cultivated plots.
We hope to see bright birds,
but see nine dingy shacks.
Some local passengers crowd on.
Brown eyes look - not at us -
but down at dusty feet.
Brown feet move quickly through
our private car in silence.

Not she -
no quiet deference for her.
Her history-honed machete voice
slashes through the door
denouncing privilege.
She cuts a path with epithets
from two strong languages.
Shouting curses down the aisle,
she argues every foot
of territory.

We see her angry face, dark brown
beneath a red bandana knotted turban style.
She clings a moment to each seat back.
Corded muscles climb her arms
sinuous as roots in shallow soil.
Window after window,
her massive shadow blots the sun.
Where there had been light talk,
a dark green silence spreads,
dense as jungle growth.

Pale arms and faces float
like rootless air plants
hovering in humid air.
The tour guide struggles at the door.
It clatters shut.
One low sigh
shudders through the car.
Then nervous laughter
flutters to the floor
like severed cane.

Past the ridge the track uncurls,
strikes for the Carib coast.
Jungle gnaws on cultivated plots.
Where we had hoped to see bright birds,
we see more dingy shacks.

MASOCHIST

She gathers guilt as though it were a gift,
cherishes the chance to willingly atone
for all imperfect world's shortcomings,
claims for herself a pardon's better half.
Her quick *"I'm sorry"* for a non-offense
transmutes a shared mistake into misdeed.
Her martyr's gluttony for penance
swallows her partner's portion,
leaves him open-mouthed and empty, denied
her hair shirt luxury of contrition.

PRECISION INSTRUMENTS

She zeroes in. Right on target. Makes another point.
Her probing needle pricks each premise, bursts
the airy argument's colorful balloons.
With logic, lean and lethal as an
ice pick or a steel-tipped dart,
she nails her opposition's
shriveled ego
dead center
bull's eye

*

Everything about her: hard and sharp.
Wiry hands chop air - karate gestures.
Blood red nails flash danger signals.
Her insistent voice, its pitch and tone,
a power saw subduing stubborn knots.
She paces as she talks, staccato steps
for emphasis. Four-inch stiletto heels
punch tiny crescents into hardwood floors.
She scissors through the fluff of fantasy.
Scrapes away the detritus of fairy dust.
Her wit, a keen-edged cleaver, slices
cleanly through trandition's toughest rind,
shreds sentiment's soft flesh, bares
the naked bone of her spare creed.
She hones and polishes each cutting edge
and he, who long has been her whetstone,
is ground thin - thinner through the years,
dwindles -
dwindles -
dwindles -
and slowly disappears.

51

CHANGELING CHILD

She does not toe the line.
That's fine.

They dance an alien beat,
those feet.

She hears a different drum
that some

can never quite recall
at all.

Yet those who strain an ear
to hear

through amplifiers of
their love

from time to time have found
a sound

from some lost time and place,
a trace

of echoes they can't yet
forget.

MY MANIC FRIEND

Quick drop from high to low?
　　　　Oh, no - not so.
That's more how elevators go.

A pendulum, she'll fly
　　　　from high to high
till something makes momentum die.

Then like an unwound clock,
　　　　tick ... tock .... tick ..... tock
gets slower from some unknown shock

And plumb bob touches ground -
　　　　profound, profound
the nadir of existence found.

Entrapped by entropy,
　　　　not free - not free
to break the hold of gravity

Some act of will occurs -
　　　　not hers - not hers.
Once more the mechanism whirs.

She will resume her ride
　　　　from side to side,
the lodestone pull denied

And she will not recall -
　　　　at all - at all
the depths, the slowing down, the fall.

ICE MAIDEN

She walks
with head held high
in frozen space
inside a boundary
invisible,
but clearly known.

She talks
in sweet low tones,
yet chilly pauses cling.
Words of welcome hang
like tender fruit
in sculptured ice.

She waits,
wanting, but wary
of west wind's warmth
and blooms beyond her season,
an orchid in acrylic
unreachable.

SCHEHERAZADE OF THE COCKTAIL LOUNGE

She laughs
too near hysteria's crystal rim,
charms him, disarms him
with a clever quote,
another bubbly anecdote.
Prays, *"Oh, happy happy hour -
let it last until once more
the fateful moment's past."*
Says, *"Yes"* and *"Yes"*
as he refills her glass.
The gassy liquid's trembling
helps her deft dissembling.
For dreaded truth
lies in the goblet's emptiness.
Each facet highlights
fragmented reflections
from one thousand other nights
of fickle fading youth
and leaves in view
the bitter residue.

MEMORABILIA

One more ragged day
trimmed and pasted down.
This is her reality
a scrapbook thing,
selected partial truths
cut to proper size.

She skims old pages,
lets snippets of life,
catalogued and labeled
come through to her
now that she has made them
neat and orderly.

The rest is discard
bits and borders
that escape her tight design.
She cannot bear
their tangled
assymetric beauty.

Saving For A Rainy Day

he does not squander
hard earned capital
banks each spare ¢
interest compounds
always + never -
$$$$$$$$$$$$$$$$s
fill narrow lines
in bank books

bolted doors
and shuttered windows
cannot block out
spendthrift neighbors
partying all night
!!!!!!!!!!!!!!!!!!!!!!!!!!!!!!s
ricochet from wall
to dimlit bedroom wall

tightly edited
single spaced
his lower case
nights and days
are deconstructed as
????????????????s
spill past the time-lock
invade his fitful dreams

for no man is a
soundproof bank vault
never ask for whom
the big box booms
a lowering cloud of
0000000000000000s
comes settling all accounts
with him   with you   with me

HAIRDRESSER

You talk to customers obliquely,
address them through your double in the glass.
You want and get, not feedback, but another hour
of non-judgmental, non-directive listening.
Sparks punctuate your mirrored sentences,
gold exclamation points.

Among those baubles, shiny tokens,
prizes from yourself and other lovers,
I fantasize a talisman hung from your neck,
a cameo with female portraits back to back:
your daughter's profile on the outer side,
your mother's at your breast.

You, who were so poorly mothered, struggle
with the task of mothering the two of them.
Both suck your thin resources dry.
You grow more brittle, transparent as the glass
you can't keep from your mother's tremored hand,
the glass your daughter used to cut her wrist.

You found your daughter on the floor, unconscious
as you found your mother other times -
but sprawled on bloodied carpet in a refuse heap
of shells, dead fish and shards of the aquarium:
the gift her sometimes Sunday father promised,
then forgot. The birthday gift you bought.

Fearful to leave her by herself,
you brought her to the shop - thin shanks
in skin-tight pants, narrow chest in tank top -
your caricature. Years stretched thin and taut
from her botched job of lipstick, blush and shadow
to your subtle palette, aged you for all your art.

You cannot tell your daughter that you love her.
Round thoughts like "care" abort to dead,
dwarfed shapes like "custody". "I love you."
such simple, sullied words. Your mother
still manages to mumble them almost too drunk
to speak, uses those three words as strategy,

fogs the target, leaves you with unspent rage.
I see a drowning child choked on unshed tears.
For all the hard-earned dollars, all the hours
you spend to baffle age, I doubt you ever look
as young as late at night, your face
turned to the wall, crying yourself to sleep.

Waving Through A
Half-Closed Window

Each day Charles smiles and waves, and so
I wave right back at him as though
we are the best of friends.
The mail drops in the box once more
and there our contact ends.

So often that it now seems funny,
I find among the pleas for money,
an ill-delivered letter
addressed to someone right next door
I hardly know much better.

Our doors, not sixty feet apart -
time after time I almost start,
that envelope in hand.
The reason that I change my mind,
I fail to understand.

Between the metal box and wall,
a tiny crack and that is all.
I take the letter. Stick it up.
The next day Charles comes 'round, he'll find
the thing and pick it up.

IV: DEFYING ZERO

"God's silence
ripens man's though
into speech."
Radindranath Tagore,
Stray Birds # 305

PEARL OF GREAT PRICE

A truth that did not fit stuck in my thought
and rasped me like a stubborn grain of sand.
No prodding with a sturdy counter-point
would pry it loose or make me understand.

To find some ease, I pushed it far below
the depth where conscious prickings shape my day,
and there unnoticed in my daily round,
it built a luminescent overlay.

And now it can be cherished as a pearl.
Its rugged hidden center I can't see
through layered coats of gentle paradox,
its harshness cushioned by a mystery.

What other better method could I use?
I would have had to build my world anew
to make accommodation for a truth
I can't accept, yet can't forget I knew.

PRAYER MEETING

Behold the Wednesday penitent
comes sheepishly through the door,
his mismatched coat and trousers
more disheveled than before -
lost lamb in cast-off woolens,
spotted, rumpled, frayed;
and just as they did those other times,
the faithful seem dismayed.

I am a budding Mary,
a dreamy twelve-year-old,
who has yet to ask the questions
which will drive me from the fold.
I shrink toward some work-worn Marthas,
away from his rank scent's reach
and smell their drug store talcum
permeated by chlorine bleach.

As he tells his wretched story,
as he bares his bleeding heart,
the stranger raises confession
to the level of oral art.
Only Grandpa in the pulpit
can rival his King James prose
as he wrestles with a devil
not one of the faithful knows.

He leaves before the final hymn
as silently as he came.
Nobody knows his address.
Nobody knows his name.
"I hope that drunk don't come no more,"
I hear one Martha say,
*"I think he's got a lotta nerve
to come here dressed that way."*

I think of the Wednesday penitent
quite often now I am grown.
Did he empty his cup of bitter wine?
Did he break his bread alone?
Was anybody a witness
on the day of his final trial?
Was he both the accused and accuser
in his self-destructive style?

Did anyone go there to mourn him?
And, if not, who is able to say
whether or not an angel came
to roll the stone away?

A LIFETIME OUT OF THE NURSERY

An old-shoe kind of faith,
glows like an Easter morning,
like scuffed-up Mary Janes
polished with a dab of vaseline
on a square of toilet tissue,
renewed with butter box insoles,
made ready for the streetcar ride
downtown to Baby Bible Class.
A now created from the remnants
of a scarce-remembered then
reaches for sky-high heaven.
My spirit, with the sun, ascends
a bold triumphant arc.
By afternoon, the press
of doubt and circumstance
deflects my flighty course.
I follow the sun's descent, drawn
by the lodestone of a lifetime's
choice for hearth's warm welcome.
Later while my day-mind sleeps,
dreamtime's busy elves sneak
through the open window,
do their industrious best
to cobble a worn illusion.

NIGHT CRY

call my name
help thou my unbelief
wake me to the sound
of sudden rain
against a dusty window

feed me with segments
of winter oranges
make me forget
the taste of ash
the taste of bile

mask the stench
of rotting flesh
with a tang of bruised mint
fragrance of windfall apples
baked with cinnamon

touch me
ever so gently
stroke my hair
massage away the tension
from my neck and shoulders

let fitful light
strike past the surface
of my darkened mirror
to reflect the image
of a trusting child

WAITING FOR LIGHTNING TO STRIKE

Do I still expect
a shaft of heaven's light
to illuminate me in a front-stage spot?

Or bushes near my path
to flame with new interpretations
of *shoulds* and *musts* intended by
that old Grandfather-Man?

Or search the constellations
for stray stars and haloed messengers
to name my name and write my destiny
in hot heraldic script on smoking walls?

I have learned of late to live
with low-watt explanations.
Helicopters beam our midnight alleys.
Scant rainfall and high creosote
torch California chapparal.

As for aureoles, there was a summertime
when I ate right, slept well,
kept all my pores and senses open,
and was convinced the radiance
that burned in me would shed a wider glow.

But I slow down and earth
spins faster on its axis,
rolls on through bright and dark.
Seasons blur and memory collages
into ambiguity of light and shadow.

On a clearing day, one distant rainbow
is enough, but fearful/hopeful
in this night of storm, I shout
a chant from childhood
surviving into post-atomic time:

one ... 1,000 ...
             two ... 1,000 ...
                      three ...

Older than Eve - older than Adam -
a beast roar echoes
and I wait for skies to split.

A GOOD FRIDAY MEDITATION

What if I chucked it all -
lock - stock - barrel,
swapped department store apparel
for saffron robe and beggar's bowl?
Would that save my jaundiced soul?

And though my fortune's rather small,
if I willed my worldly goods
to L.A.'s blighted neighborhoods,
would my mirror show that I
had traversed the needle's eye?

Would a sacrificial fire
to burn my last remaining cash
and empty purse as so much trash,
be the trick to find the key
for entering eternity?

What if I quenched my last desire,
entered each dawning day afresh
devoid of pleasures of the flesh,
would history take me for a saint,
remember me for what I ain't?

Suppose I really did these things,
but then was greeted by the shock,
none of my keys would turn the lock
to let me through the pearly gate
and I would have to sit and wait

hearing a whir of angel's wings
beyond the wall I could not breach,
paradise still out of reach,
then hear St. Pete pontificate:
"far too little - much too late."

A CHRISTMAS QUESTIONER

One night? One star?
Did angels sing
for birth apart
from everything?
Event discrete?
Long past? Afar?
With no repeat
but echoing?
Or is the spark
in each beginning
of light from dark
a holy thing?
Would wisdom bring
us gifts we need,
the open hearts,
to heed the beat
of angel wings -
here - where we are?

A Prayer For Understanding
By One Of The Unredeemed

Each time I think of Calvary, I see
the forest, not the one symbolic tree,
and I am mystified.
How could another crucified
atone for all the world condemns to die?

I shun the gilded shrines where I could pray,
repelled by the reputed part You play.
not failure of the flock.
Your hand-picked prisoner at the block
is why I keep my unbowed head up high.

Dear God, I cannot think a shepherd nice
who breeds a lamb intent on sacrifice.
Was that Your true intention:
the plot those theologians mention
or grievous errors of the unenlightened?

Perhaps an angry patriarchal Hebrew
confused an obscure message sent by You.
If daughters had been heard,
perhaps a less bloodthirsty word
could now be read by us, but I am frightened

this notion too is idle speculation.
I've heard the shrill-voiced cry for vindication.
What hope for better text
by zealots alternately sexed,
for vixens can be every bit as cruel.

Prayer for Understanding
by One of the Unredeemed

I would not want sad sisters on my jury.
I've seen their tarantella full of fury
demanding as Salome
a bearded head upon a tray.
No, I would be an atavistic fool

to think a gender-generated creed
would be the one to fill my reverent need
for more than might makes right
and children's fear-filled prayers at night
learned in some misguided Sunday School.

CAVERNS

Time is a cavern.
If you go far enough
in any direction,
you find a deep pool
where no-color fish
circle dark water
in blind perfection,
one continuous arc
around and around

Silence - a cavern
where a spoken word
spawns myriad echoes,
complex choreography -
a disciplined darting
of miniscule plankton
drawn into the maw
of a great white whale
who emits no sound

Sleep is a cavern,
a blood-dark womb
sheltering, nourishing
with impartial care
monsters or heroes,
demons or demigods
bred from the union -
egg of remembrance.
sperm of desire.

Tradition is cavern,
a sanctified tomb
where the ancestors lie
and young are taken
through pain to joy
to see totem animals
revealed on the wall
in uncertain light
of ritual fire.

Religion is cavern,
an ache in the dark
for a cleft in the rock
of an empty all -
a temple, a mosque
a gothic cathedral,
cold stone floors
stained with gem-tone
luminescence.

Art is a cavern,
labyrinthine quest
for the source of light,
turn after turn
out of stygian dark
into stygian dark,
lured by a glimmer
of glowworm
phosphorescence.

Mind is a cavern,
a nautilus shell,
spiral passage,
smal dark cells,
briny memory,
pull of the tides,
hum of a conch,
rough exterior,
hidden opalescence.

MYTHMAKING

How many times have I been told
                    ours is a winter world?

How many times am I reminded
                    our sun is a dying star?

   There are times my mirror and my calendar
   foretell that all I know draws to a close,
   days I rage my part is late and small,
   nights I cry and argue with my fate

        one more abandoned hope,
        another dear friend lost,
        an ebb of energy,
        an ache, a new complaint,
        some limit to my strength,
        a lapse of memory

when
      I find release in wintry imagery.
      Dark harmonies of loss, decay and cold
      let me pretend   with grand significance
      I am not crying for myself alone.

I like to call this clever fit

      of mind and mood and history:

                    my tragic destiny!

But other times all signs are right:
stars in auspicious houses, temperature benign,
barometric pressure optimum,
work going well
       digestion good
            joints moving freely

when
       a laugh, a face, a flower,
       a new friend lately found,
       fresh bread and fragrant wine,
       a melody, a metaphor,
       the scent of ripened oranges,
       the warmth of skin on skin

rescues some live core of self from history,
nets me from my dying fall, suspends me
webbed by fragile bonds in some rare altitude

where
       eons are compacted in one heartbeat.
       vision, unbound by time, mimics omniscience
       to watch through insect -
               serpent -
                   eagle eyes

infinite young worlds expand and multiply.

I like to call
this strange identity
of mind and mood
and mystery:

Eternity

PENUMBRA

Not all pre-dawn glimmer
is sucked at once
into a rising sun.
Some clings to a beloved face,
an aureole more sensed
than seen.

A hand reaches
from scattered sleep
for pen and scratch pad
hoping to catch
a fading ray
of dream light.

The eyes,
the skin
of some light-headed
hunger striker
at the barricade
cast a widening glow.

Near a grayed
cell window,
a martyr wakes
and with a stubby pencil
marks off another date
on a grimy calendar.

Each lover
beckoned to,
driven by
a dimly heard
and star-begotten
word

MATIN

Sometimes,
lack of sleep will do it.
Nights of new-discovered love,
conversation long past midnight
with a destined friend,
nursing a newborn infant,
tending a convalescing child
or chosen work become
more meaningful than rest
will open me to morning sun.

For a while I glow,
an east-facing stained glass window
ingesting God and sunrise.
Perceptive eyes might penetrate
translucent skin, see veins and arteries
transparent tubes of neon,
watch vital organs strobe gem tones
over intricate skeletal sculpture,
a gleam of old ivory
and rare white jade.

And I remember
what I never will forget:
a long-ago first time
the child I was
help up an open hand
against the morning sun
to discover my so-solid body
to be, after all,
nothing more and nothing less
than halo and shadow.

A Triptych Of Angels

Visiting Churches in Italy

I:

I learned these legends
in a storefront church
larger than a manger, but
smaller than a barn,
bare of decoration,
workshed plain.
Its low stained ceiling
didn't stop my angel
hovering in Sunday air
or my imagination
feathering its wings
in iridescence.
Although I had not seen
St. Peter's or St. Mark's,
I knew that rainbows
shimmer around the throats
of pigeons strutting
in the city parks.

II.

Nuns in heavy habits of black cloth
hover near a marble plaque
engraved with some dead pontiff's name.
Two robust angels, lightly draped,
lean seductively toward numerals
that flank a hyphen, one small minus mark
to signify the time his spirit occupied
its home of flesh. A century ago,
some unnamed craftsman incised angelic curves
full enough to grace a centerfold of *Playboy Magazine*.
Do dark-clad sisters think
this is a proper way
to venerate a celibate?

Blond hairs glid muscled legs
of German boys in skimpy shorts -
and I almost put on my jacket
in spite of summer heat
out of deference to Baedeker:
*"Appropriate clothing should be worn
when visiting churches."*

There is tension in this Roman temple
of issues not yet decided.
Do we lose paradise because of naked flesh
or through our uncalled-for shame of it?
I choose the side of angels
as did Michelangelo
400 years ago.

III.

In the bigger churches
with guides and audio-visual aids,
parades of visitors, not penitents,
who come like us to worship
sculptured marble, gilded bronze,
and frescoed walls by famous names,
an old conundrum echoed:

> *How many angels*
> *find room enough to dance*
> *on the head of a common pin?*

I could not hear an answer
in the din of many voices.

In San Miniato Al Monte
with simple jars of ripened wheat
before each station of the cross,
I heard the question once again.
One of the faithful knelt in prayer.
We two, the only strangers there,
walked softly, did not speak.
In the hush, I heard the answer plain:

> *Every angel man has dreamt before,*
> *each angel man now dreams,*
> *and room left for one angel more -*
> *always room left for one more.*

TIME OUT OF MIND

The Greeks said Cronus ate his children raw,
so cryogenicists hope Father Time
will pass them by if they take long to thaw.

Perhaps you think it's bordering on crime -
or even worse - committing venal sin
to make a jest of matters as sublime

as life and death; but if I can't begin
to poke the ribs of my mortality,
fate's played a joke on me that I can't win.

This shell of individually,
destined from the first as dust to dust,
conceals some alternate modality -

a point of view in which I have to trust.
I'd weep if nothing lasts beyond the grave.
We heavy thinkers laugh because we must

and not because we're stoical and brave.
The story said, though Cronus was a lout,
his goodwife Gaea forced him to behave.

Those early Greeks knew what they were about.
He spat his undigested offspring out.

AGNOSTIC'S PRAYER

(after George Herbert's *The Temper*)

Dear God, if You exist and if You care,
If more was asked and I gave less,
Forgive and let me claim my share
Of sloth and idleness:

Those wasted times when I congratulate
Myself on daydreams of intent;
Do much too little, much too late,
Enthusiasm spent.

Forgive those deeds that cannot be undone:
Brazen bending, callous breaking,
When I have been the guilty one
Of any greedy taking.

If choices I have made were wholly free,
Forgive my careless choosing;
If greater goals were meant for me
And I chose losing.

I'll dwell within this edifice of guilt,
Repent until my unknown ending,
If that is the abode I've built
Without defending

My faults and failed potentiality.
I'll pay whatever cost is due
And not project fatality
On hypothetic You.

Release me from the world of randomness,
A life that often seems absurd.
I need, much more than Your forgiveness,
A reassuring word.

Show me how to be a child once more.
If that is what it takes for me
To feel Your nearness as before
My long apostasy.

Help me with the awesome task of living.
Quell my proud and anxious heart.
Free me from this dark misgiving
That idle prayers depart

To emptiness along with all I love.
But if this dread is true, why then
Do I keep sending words above
Addressed to You?   Amen.

WIND CHIMES

I.   *L.A.'s Second Chinatown*

Herbs, roots, bones in apothecary jars,
exotic foodstuffs for the locals,
Taiwan gimcracks for the tourist trade,
the store was in a narrow alley
away from the false front Broadway entrance
toward the more authentic Hill Street side.
The children thought the shop was ancient.
My father took me into older stores
the Union Station crowded out
with open bins of lichee nuts, dried ginger,
plucked ducks and chickens hung by scaly feet.
A relocated tradesman must have brought
his large extended family's sepia past
and the windchimes hung above the counter,
translucent glass turned fossil amber.
Each gust from the opened street door
renewed the pendant's spiral dance,
faint echoes of a Chinese crescent's bells,
and some other half-remembered music
from another time and place.

II. *Food For The Savage Gods*

We purchased cookies to take home,
fatty disks with shiny almond omphalos,
ignored the risk of arteries blocked
the way invading tourist traffic clogged
these narrow stone-paved alleys,
Before the bag was full, oil oozed
dark brown spots on light brown paper.
The wind chimes played their temple call.
Perhaps before one eats celebratory food,
one should make offerings to appease
devouring gods of hunger and abundance,
anoint abandoned altars with libations
of rare old wine and sanctified oil.
We made our way back to the plaster fountain.
Our tossed pennies, other coins, orange carp
reflected a shattered late-day sun
through littered, rippled water.
Memory fragments shifted, churned
like shards of broken shells tumbling
in the surge and suck of waves.
I had heard music of La Jolla tide pools
in the amber windchimes' tinkling song - heard
music from the orient in crevices, small caverns
of eroded Southern California littoral.

III.   *Gift On A Crowded Shelf*

My oldest son, with an artist's ear and eye
for chance-found beauty, made some excuse,
returned and bargained with the merchant,
spent his week's allowance, one crumpled U.S. dollar,
gave me his unwrapped gift in an old cigar box.
We both had known the lovely amber was patina:
fumes from cars and busses, dusty indoor air
heavy with wok-warmed oil - peanut, soya, sesame.
Faint marks on the glass rectangles
were not the Chinese characters we'd thought,
but abstract leaves and flowers, squiggles and strokes
most likely painted in some piece work sweat shop.
He did not know some of the rust-orange strings
tied to the metal rings and glued to the glass
by small circles of tarnished foil had rotted through,
or how long I would keep my treasure unrepaired
buried in clutter on a linen closet shelf.

By chance, between foregettings,
I come across the box - MADE IN TAMPA
in gilt block letters on a scrolled black banner -
on the inside lid, TAMPA NEEDLES-SHREDDED-HAVANA
LONG FILLER - HAND ROLLED - 5 ¢ STRAIGHT.
I lift the windchimes gently, glass plates jangle.
I think how the Atlantic must cudgel and caress
the coasts of Florida, Cuba and the misnamed West Indies
till shattered shells respond with music.

IV.   *La Jolla Tide Pools*

On slippery rock at land's edge, I listen
to the amniotic wash of the Pacific,
the *chaconne* of pastel shells.
Out of their watery element,
those jewel-toned shards bleach white,
the skeletal white of brine, or bird lime.
Small pools swirl with small crustaceans
feeding on miniscule organisms.
I hear a dissonant cry, watch a gull
wheel, dive, rise, a morsel in its beak.
That's what it is about, isn't it?
Life feeding on life - sun, wind, tide
breaking up earth's old configurations,
making new-found compositions - and yet,
some of my kind with ear to conch,
spiral shell to spiral shell,
have heard the rich prophetic OM
not fragmented into the wrangling voices
of devouring gods of hunger and abundance.
We try to hear a voice behind the voices -
listening, telling of the listening -
and in the doing, we too break patterns,
compose new patterns from old fragments
with care one does not tear the tap root,
the long umbilical.

CRATER LAKE

The first time I saw Crater Lake,
I quit looking for final answers,
began a long slow letting-go
of preconceptions, expectations,
the puzzle over unreflected worlds
behind the Rorschäch blot
on everything:

> my broomstick witches,
> your ballerinas,
> your bats from hell,
> my butterflies.
> Whether we admit it or not,
> each of us has seen
> the empty staring skull,
> pelvic bones or rib cage -
> our private, hidden skeleton
> drawn x-ray plain
> stark black on white.

Crater Lake, my still point.
Trees grow head first into aquamarine,
Clouds drift in green-black water.
I go there from the dentist's chair,
from pap smear torture stirrups,
for brief amnesia from no-exit grief.
With this retreat, I can make do.
I am unready for *if I die before I wake*,
white light at the end of the tunnel,
or to face the faceless mirror.
I am content to muse on reflections
floating floating in deep water.

NORTH ON THE 605

Clear now from smog and haze,
my flat foreshortened vision
opens out and up, climbs foothills
glitter-green from recent rains,
scales chiseled planes and hollows,
deep blues and deeper purples -
perspective on perspective,
five distinct mountain ridges
shawled in scalloped snow.
Reflections from a puffy patch
of dawn-pink cumulus
brush faintest rose across
Mt. Baldy's slopes.

This January morning,
I can almost ignore
the gray and gritty foreground:
pot-holed asphalt,
oil-stained concrete,
tangled steel-wire mesh,
on-ramps, off-ramps, parking lots,
careless casual clutter
of small scale industry,
ragged ravaged gravel pits.

In Southern California,
this too-brief season
is our winter and our spring.
Emerging out of fumes and failures,
reprieved from grime and greed,
the beauty of the land
lets me believe once more
in ancient promises
of forgiveness
and a new beginning.

UROBOROS

Do you hear the circle closing?
That sibilant sound?
The hiss of the serpent
reaching for his flailing tail?

Hear sighs of solipsist seers
contemplating their navels:
those small circular scars
of the first separation?

How long will whispered questions
be unheard in the clamorous racket
of the barricade builders
enclosing the next walled city?

When the line without an end
meets the line with no beginning,
won't lovers dreamers poets
climb the stony parapet, find

embrasures left for marksmen
windows onto the open
and watch the slivered moon
slowly ripen to a silver round?

Behold configurations forming
in spaces between the farthest stars?
Map a zodiac of new-discovered gods
from stardust at vision's outer edge?

Spend wakeful nights in wonder
until darkness dissipates
and the fiery disk of the sun
brightens a green horizon

to an aubade of bird-song?.
See sparrow and winged shadow
in twinned flight over grassy ground
toward a stand of olive trees?

And know the world beyond the wall
holds nests of ovoid promise
of unhatched possibility
defying zero?

ABOUT THE BOOK:

I wish to give special thanks to my granddaughter, Jennifer Heywood Smithson, Imagine Graphics, her Huntington Beach, California company, served as Book Designer and Producer for this collection of poems. Jennifer's encouragement, patience and skill guided this work through the computerization and printing processes.

I want to thank Robert Smithson, my grandson-in-law, for the artwork on the cover, title and divider pages. He created a version of a mandala and squared circle with an expanding center almost, but not completely, obscuring an underlying dark circle of nothingness.

I also want to give thanks to Dr. Jack Fulbeck, Professor Emeritus of English Literature of California Polytechnic University at Pomona. A good poet and good friend, he gave an earlier draft of this work a careful reading and made detailed comments. Many of these were greatly helpful and led to revisions of certain poems. Others were ignored due to the idiosyncrasies and personal preferences of this poet. I am certain Jack, a widely-read and opened-minded critic, understands that final choices belong to and are the sole responsibility of the author.

ABOUT THE AUTHOR:

ELAINE LAZZERONI

was born Grace Elaine Mason in Los Angeles, California in 1920. After a journalism course at Los Angeles City College, she transferred to the University of California at Berkeley. In 1942, she received a Phi Beta Kappa key, a B.A., in Social Institutions (a department of social theory no longer in existence), and married to Ivo Lazzeroni. In 1968 when the youngest of four children was thirteen, she received a Master's Degree in Sociology from California State University at Los Angeles. She chose this field of study largely due to the fact that no prerequisites other than courses taken during undergraduate work would be required.

She began employment as a social worker for Los Angeles County in 1969. Several poems in this collection grew out of experience working in the General Relief and Adult Protective Services programs. Although she has written poetry (off and on) since childhood, she did not share poetry with others until after retirement in 1982. She resides in West Covina, California with her husband.